Seasons

"CELEBRATIONS IN THE LIFE OF THE CHURCH"

VOCAL SOLO (MEDIUM RANGE)

CONTENTS

MUSIC ENGRAVING BY TOM McANINCH
DESIGN BY DIANE JACOBS

Seasons

KMP2004 (Book only)   KMP2004CD (Book/CD pack)

Visit Hal Leonard Online at www.halleonard.com
Visit Phillip Keveren at www.phillipkeveren.com
Visit Steve Siler at www.musicforthesoul.org

Keveren MUSIC PRESS

EXCLUSIVELY DISTRIBUTED BY
HAL•LEONARD® CORPORATION
7777 W. BLUEMOUND RD. P.O. BOX 13819 MILWAUKEE, WI 53213

2

PREFACE

Music, like no other God-given gift, can touch us in a special way. When the Church Family comes together in celebration, nothing like a song better expresses our feelings, emotions, hopes and desires. It distills our thoughts and focuses our minds on the occasion at hand. Such music can be, as the song says, a blessing from our Lord.

Steve Siler and I wrote these songs in the autumn of 2003. My family had recently entered a new season in our lives, having moved from California to Tennessee. Steve gave me much enouragement at that time, and creating these compositions together brought great joy.

We hope these songs will provide a moment of inspiration in the life of your church.

In His Service,

Phillip Keveren

Phillip Keveren

BIOGRAPHIES

Phillip Keveren is co-author, major composer and MIDI orchestrator of the internationally acclaimed *Hal Leonard Student Piano Library*. His stylish piano arrangements are featured in *The Phillip Keveren Series* (Hal Leonard).

Phillip has arranged and orchestrated for many recording artists in the Christian music field, including Twila Paris, Larnelle Harris, Bob Carlisle, John Tesh, Greg Long and Scott Krippayne.

Steve Siler is the writer of "Circle of Friends", "Not Too Far From Here", "I Will Follow Christ", and many other well-known Christian songs. He has nine number-one songs, 35 top-ten singles, and a Dove Award for Inspirational song of the year to his credit.

Steve is Executive Director of Music for the Soul, a non-profit company that creates music for people dealing with issues of recovery, and he is the author of The Praise & Worship Devotional (Tyndale House).

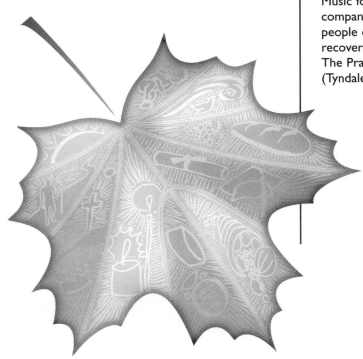

Advent

Light of the World

Words & Music by
Phillip Keveren & Steve Siler

Communion

At This Table

Words and Music by
Phillip Keveren & Steve Siler

Marriage

When Two Become One

(Male/Female Duet)

Words and Music by
Phillip Keveren & Steve Siler

Male (8vb): From the start___ of time,___ it was meant___ to be:___ two dif - f'rent lives,___ one pre - fect des - ti - ny.___

Risen

Words and Music by
Phillip Keveren & Steve Siler

Graduation

Let Jesus Be Your Guide

Words and Music by
Phillip Keveren & Steve Siler

In ev - 'ry - thing, let Je - sus be_____ your guide.

The world_____ meas - ures suc - cess by wealth and pow - er,

and no one knows_____ just how much is_____ e -

Baptism

Streams of Living Water

Words and Music by
Phillip Keveren & Steve Siler

Until We Meet Again

Words and Music by
Phillip Keveren & Steve Siler

Memorial

We Celebrate Your Life

Words and Music by
Phillip Keveren & Steve Siler

Thanksgiving

Blessing from Our Lord

Words and Music by
Phillip Keveren & Steve Siler

Baby Dedication

New Hope for the World

Words and Music by
Phillip Keveren & Steve Siler